HUMILITY vs. HUMILIATION

About the pamphlet:
Compulsive overeaters have conditioned themselves to expect humiliation. Without careful attention, recovering overeaters might recreate the same pain and degradation in other areas of their daily lives, simply because they know nothing else. This pamphlet suggests how to walk away from situations that put down and belittle, and toward those which nourish and encourage.

About the author:
Dr. Judi Hollis has been treating addicted families since 1968, and currently specializes in developing hospital eating disorder units, and the HOPE Institute (Helping Overeaters thru People and Education). An international lecturer on problems of addiction, she appears regularly on radio and television and is author of the book, *Fat is a Family Affair,* and several pamphlets published by Hazelden Educational Materials. She lives in Hermosa Beach, California.

HUMILITY vs. HUMILIATION

JUDI HOLLIS, Ph.D.

First published February, 1986.

ISBN: 0-89486-359-2

Printed in the United States of America.

Editor's Note:
   Hazelden Educational Materials offers a variety of information on chemical dependency and related areas. Our
publications do not necessarily represent Hazelden or its
programs, nor do they officially speak for any Twelve Step
organization.

There is no person, place, or thing big enough to make me small enough to take that first compulsive bite.

I SUFFER, THEREFORE I AM

Are you ready to give up the suffering? You've probably already suffered enough. Filled with self-loathing and depression, you may blame yourself for an illness you didn't create or ask to have. If you are like most compulsive overeaters, you've lived a lifetime of failed attempts at control, and broken promises to yourself and others. If nothing else, you know how to suffer.

René Descartes philosophized, "I think, therefore I am," but the overeater believes, "I suffer, therefore I am." We are people who can snatch defeat from the jaws of victory. If the food doesn't knock us to our knees, we will teach other people to humiliate and degrade us to recreate our old desperate feelings. One of my patients reported, "I never felt so alive as when I was being ridiculed and degraded. My fingers would tingle and my heart would pound." It is as if the pain of suffering is the proof of being real.

RECOVERY: A DIFFERENT REALITY

Recovering from an eating disorder involves learning to go for the good life with gusto. Instead of competing and evaluating ourselves on a grandiose scale of our own making, we can begin to live real lives by developing a *realistic* sense of ourselves. In recovery, we learn to accept ourselves as we are and to live in the here and now. We will start by slowing down and accepting "progress, not perfection." We will come to truly believe *we are enough.* We may have spent a lifetime feeling abnormal and deformed, and our freakishness attracted negative attention. This has been stardom on a humiliating stage. We may be so accustomed to enduring jeers, teasing, judgmental stares, and finger-pointing lectures that the comfort of degradation is hard to give up. At least we

1

know what to expect. It's not that we enjoy the suffering, it's that we know nothing else.

Rosa recognized this when she saw her first and only bullfight.

"It was devastating, not because they killed the bull, but because they teased him. They kept taunting: pulling, poking, and laughing. The bull kept fighting for his life as though there was a chance. He had to fight; there was nothing else to do, even though it was fruitless. The bull would have to suffer and die. He suffered humiliation before the hooting crowd as its insensitive, drugged entertainment. There was no sensitivity to the plight of the bull. It must have been very lonely. As the carcass was dragged away at last, there was relief for the bull and exultation for a crowd which had lost its senses."

The taunting, the humiliation, and the painful, incomprehensible demoralization of the overeater corresponds magnificently to the suffering of the bull. In recovery, without careful attention, we can recreate the same pain and degradation emblazoned on us from earliest memory. Recovery will necessitate our walking away from situations that put down and belittle us, and toward those which nourish and encourage us.

Eating disorder sufferers are described as egomaniacs with inferiority complexes. Negotiating the delicate balance between foolish pride and false humility is a precarious venture in recovery. The Twelve Steps are an ego-deflating program which proposes moderation in all things. Rigorous honesty with ourselves about who we are is crucial to our recovery. We are as fat as we are dishonest. True humility is an honest recognition of our assets and liabilities without judging ourselves. Some of us try to ward off our egotism by lapsing into false humility, assuming self-deprecating stances. Some people find it hard to accept compliments and shy away from any special attention. They won't call a sponsor, afraid they'll "bother" or "impose." Others are extremely defensive about

2

their defects or liabilities and deny them vehemently. They offer rationalizations, putting others on the defensive. In all honesty, no one is better or worse than anyone else; we each have our own row to hoe. Most truly humble individuals are not even aware of their humility. If you're sure you are humble, you're probably not.

GET AWAY FROM MY PLATE

The very first conflicts with our egos come with our struggles in negotiating abstinence. It is crucial that we are abstinent when we confront our ego systems. This is a two-edged sword. We need the sense of well-being and moderate discipline that abstinence brings before looking closely at character defects, or we might feel so bad about ourselves that we won't be willing to take an honest look. This is the failure of traditional psychotherapy, which assumes that while you are still bingeing you will be able to examine your life.

Abstinence gets us to the starting gate. Involving someone else in the INTIMACY of what we decide to eat is a way to feel truly humbled by the cunning, baffling, and powerful food game. As you start to negotiate with another person what and how you are eating, you will see how truly OMNIPOTENT food has become to you. How important is it that you have that baked potato? How deprived do you feel when you've paid for an "all you can eat" buffet but choose to make only one trip through the line? Surrendering to that reality will help you surrender with dignity to other things in your life which "got the best of ya." Surrendering your food enables you to develop a more realistic view of yourself and your life without the false bravado of trying to look good.

Suzanne experienced the Twelve Steps as an ego-deflating device in her first week of abstinence. She had just created an oft-repeated household crisis. She had known for weeks that something in her washing machine needed fixing, but she let it pass and ate instead. It was during her first week of abstinence that the washer finally broke, sending torrents of suds throughout the kitchen and family room. She had just finished lunch but was still starving. (The idea of even slightly limiting her food intake felt like starvation.)

She had complained to a binge buddy after her first O.A. meeting, "Who do those folks think they are? They must be kidding! No one like me can possibly eat like that. Don't they know who they're dealing with?"

For overeaters, the idea of following ANY food plan feels like a violation, an infringement of personal freedom, persecution, and worst of all, CONTROL. We rail, "I don't see why I have to let anyone know what I'm eating. It's no one else's business!"

In the midst of just such thoughts, starving, and with two screaming small children; Suzanne called her sponsor. She yelled into the receiver, "If someone doesn't come over here right now, I'm going to eat the refrigerator and beat these kids!" Suzanne's sponsor was a mild-mannered older woman, with a sing-song lilt to her soft-spoken voice. She answered patiently in her kindest and sweetest tone, "I'm sorry, dear, I am eating my lunch right now and will have to call you back in about twenty minutes. I hope that will be all right. Perhaps you could call someone else in the meantime."

Suzanne was incensed. "That bitch! What nerve! I humbled myself by calling. I'm not eating and I need help NOW! How does she have the nerve to EAT while my world is crumbling? My drama is more important than her lunch! I might as well eat."

For some reason, however, Suzanne didn't eat but called a washer repairman instead. While he rushed over, she went to her room and wrote her feelings down. Oddly enough, her rage and hunger subsided within twenty minutes and she felt so calm she began to giggle. She actually laughed at the way she must have looked and sounded. She was now able to view her situation as quite comical. It really was funny to see that stream of white foam envelop her kitchen. When the repairman arrived, she pointed him toward the kitchen and went to call her sponsor. By that time Suzanne was obviously much calmer, still abstinent, and now she had her sponsor's undivided attention. (The twenty minutes had also allowed time for her lunch to be digested.) Both Suzanne and her sponsor noticed how quickly the compulsion to eat had subsided with some self-discipline and a little writing. Suzanne had to laugh with joy at having made it through a crisis without turning to food.

Behavior modification research indicates that most compulsions last for about twenty minutes. If we can wait it out that seemingly *interminable* time, the compulsion passes. Most people even forget what aggravation they were about to eat over. The only way to learn how truly unnecessary the act of compulsive eating can be is to resist the urge in the midst of the turmoil. Abstinence brings perspective. Then you see how quickly you can move on to something else, sometimes even with a little smile. O.A.s are consoled with the idea that *this too shall pass,* and that nothing tastes as good as abstinence feels.

Our struggles have to be witnessed by another human being to demystify and bring them into truer perspective. If you secretly eat over feelings, minor skirmishes loom as large, ominous battles. Petty annoyances become ready avenues for self-abuse and punishment with more food. It is liberating to forgo the food for a good laugh instead.

SUCCESS IS A SPIRITUAL EXPERIENCE

Losing weight is not the problem — keeping it off is. How many times have we heard that one before? National statistics on weight loss programs attest to the truth of this statement. Of all those who have undertaken a weight loss regimen, 97 percent regain all their lost weight *and more* within two years. That means that over the long haul, and despite the fact that most people are initially "successful" weight losers, this illness shows only a three percent recovery rate! The problem is not the journey; it is the destination. How can we be successful, happy, thin, and *endure* the good life? God, grant me the serenity to endure my blessings. . . .

The problem of regaining weight is related to an inability to accept the success the O.A. program brings. Initially inspired and turned on by the success stories, the newcomer takes on abstinence with a vengeance. As overeaters, we live in a lifelong dress rehearsal for the day we are thin and our lives perfect. Such unrealistic expectations of what life will be like when we are thin lead us straight back to where we were. A successful recovery program involves a realistic attitude about problems other than food. How about the difficulties of ordinary living? If we've always lived with food as our problem, we probably haven't developed tools for handling concerns other than our diets. We haven't learned yet how to be "out among 'em" in the world. We do know how to be a fat person on a diet. We know how to be a person "starting." We've just never learned how to be or stay a "finisher."

HUMILITY IS NOT THINKING LESS OF MYSELF, BUT THINKING OF MYSELF LESS!

Some of us hang on to our food problems or abuse ourselves with lovers, money, work, or play as a way of avoiding the real possibility of becoming really "happy, joyous, and free." When so much of our lives have been spent suffering, it is difficult to go for the good life with gusto. There are certain stresses of success which many of us seek to avoid.

With success in all areas of life, what will we find to talk about? We might find old friends desert us. Without problems, what do we share in common? If we are no longer suffering and dependent, we may find it lonely at the top. That's why O.A.s recommend sticking with the winners. We must be with people who wish us well and encourage our continued success.

Some of us are afraid others will envy our new good lives and accuse us of trying to show others up. Mae West once quipped, "The worst thing is, you're not trying to show them up, you don't even know they're there." We must be able to move out of humiliation and not worry about those who want to stay back and feel abandoned by our journey. We can invite them along, we can wish them well, but we can't go back so they'll have company.

We must come to believe that God does not want us to be humiliated and suffering. Accepting success as God's gift rather than their own reward, many in O.A. become willing to recover. They can't take personal credit. They do it with God's help. They declare, "God don't make no junk." Continuing to suffer in the face of opportunity is, in a way, a slap in God's face. Success is luck that has said its prayers, and you can't duck your luck.

AW, SHUCKS

Some are overcome by the compliments and expectations of recovery. Still believing they are unworthy, they try to retreat to inadequacy rather than live up to their potential. One patient reported, "My potential almost killed me!" When so much support comes instead of criticism, it is hard to take. Well-meant compliments are often threatening, as the success-ful weight loser feels unmasked and violated by this new visibility. Some men wear beards well into recovery just to hide their faces. Women wear long hair pulled over their eyes to stay hidden. Sometimes, moving down to the smaller sizes on the clothes rack can bring back five pounds we had lost.

Hopefully, this fall from grace will be caught at five pounds, not twenty-five! With weight regained, the overeater can again feel humiliation and self-loathing. Continually failing keeps us from facing the discomfort of really chang-ing. Many fear that if they do well, success will be expected from them on a regular basis. Rather than face these expectations, they put themselves down and diminish their gifts.

If we continue to fail at abstinence regularly, it's probably because our energy is going into failing. Just by the law of averages, we have a 50-50 chance. If we fail more than half the time, it's probably because we are committed to failure. Some drive themselves to fail 95 percent of the time. Imagine that work rechanneled into recovery!

Being a perfect failure is just as dishonest as always succeeding. Everyone has bad days, and big kids do cry. No matter what is in our past, we have the same chances of making it as anyone else. Those who object and say they are unworthy, inadequate, or just "can't" are really giving in to their egotism. The perfect failure is the other side of the coin tossed by the rigid perfectionist. It is glorification of the failed ego as opposed to accepting the good things God has in store.

You may be afraid you won't know how to be YOU living the good life. You don't need to worry. You won't be given more than you can handle: you'll only be given what you are ready for. A newcomer explained to her sponsor, "I know I stay fat because I'm afraid to get thin." The sponsor replied, "Well, why don't you get thin and then we'll talk about it? For now, it's really none of your business. Your job in recovery is to suit up and show up." It makes no difference what others want to see. You will find out how to be a purely successful YOU: you will be shown the way.

None of us knows how to be a new real person until we are given the situation and the opportunity to practice. That does not mean buying a myth or image of who we think we *should* be. It means waiting with faith to see WHO shows up. A TV interviewer once told Gloria Steinem, "You sure don't look fifty years old!" She responded, "This is what fifty looks like." Gloria had to turn fifty before she could know what it looked and felt like for her. There are no rules. A startled fan, upon meeting Picasso, exclaimed, "Are you really *Picasso?*" The famous artist smiled, "I'm *almost* Picasso."

USE YOUR ABUSE

Facing the former commitment to humiliation is the first step toward change. The only way out is through. We can't avoid how bad it's been; but we can use our scars to achieve a super recovery. The O.A. program shows a way to accept how bad it's been and to make a commitment to change right here and now. It is a chance to completely change old programming and to actually be reborn to a new life within this lifetime. It is not avoiding truth or forgetting the past; it is using where we've been as a tool to get us where we are going. The dues we've paid are a part of what we have going for us. Our past failures can make us winners. *They are an asset.*

By the time we come to O.A., we've paid the price! Perhaps that price was stretch marks, back problems, hospitalizations, diabetes, surgery, divorce. Whatever it has been, we will now use events from our lives as our means to grow. The Hindus say the events of your own life are grist for the mill. "Honor your incarnation." You don't have to go to a mountaintop in Tibet; you can achieve recovery in downtown Des Moines.

What was once a mark of pain and suffering can now be worn as a badge of courage. Like the Phoenix, a bird which consumed itself by fire, only to rise anew from the ashes, you will fall apart, only to rise into a new life born from the old pain. You must use, not analyze, your past. Figuring it all out can keep you stuck in it. Take what you can use and leave the rest. Alfred Hitchcock, famous director of scary movies, said, "My greatest luck was to have been born a really frightened person." He faced and used his fear in a way that propelled him into success.

FINDING A HEALTHY NEUTRALITY

Since our greatest humiliations occurred around food, our recovery will involve approaching abstinence not as deprivation, but as dignity. If abstinence is "guilt-free eating," we need to pay attention to both the *what* and the *how* of substances in the mouth. It is not enough to develop a committed food plan with measured portions and planned meal times. The RELATIONSHIP with food has to change. That means the manner in which we take in food has to move from loathsome gorging to a refined and dignified approach. We want to eat with humility, not humiliation. The body is our temple, and food is fuel to stoke our engines.

It is possible to approach food with dignity. We need to develop a healthy neutrality. The key is to become aware of how loudly the food is calling. If it is a loud cry, if it's calling you by name, if it demands you right now or else, that's when you must leave it. When you can take it or leave it, that's when you can have it. Even when you're not eating, you can lose dignity giving excess attention to food. Are you or others embarrassed by your piranha-like feeding frenzies?

Marsha was dining out with friends who didn't want their rolls or dessert. She panicked and loudly ordered the waitress to pack it all up to "take home for the kids." Then she nervously explained how much her children liked the rolls from this restaurant. "Not for me, of course," she said. Even if she had honestly intended to take the food home to her children, the obsessive way she shouted orders divulged the extent of her addictive panic around food. Normal people are not obsessed with either getting or leaving food; it is a neutral substance. Program literature promises us we will neither be drawn to it nor swear off it. We will achieve a position of neutrality accompanied by humility.

COURTING MR. WRONG

If they are not degrading themselves at the dinner table, many compulsive overeaters will move their gorging, guzzling mentalities into their bedrooms. They may initially seek sexual contact to make up for lost time, but later use sex as a way to be put down. These people would strongly identify with the heroine of the movie, *Looking for Mr. Goodbar.* A respected professional by day, she haunted the bars and back alleys of New York City by night. Despite the fact that a nice guy was crazy about her, she became addicted to a relationship with a street hood who abused her and threatened violence. She was eventually murdered by a man she picked up in a bar after she demeaned and provoked him. Parts of this true story are retold by hundreds of overeaters in recovery. Many trade food abuse for another form of intimate violation.

Ali had been dating the same Mr. Wrong for a year and a half into her recovery. He was both abusive and demeaning. He criticized her constantly and openly flirted with other women so Ali could see. When she told him it hurt, he said she was "silly" and suggested she "see a shrink for your inferiority complex and paranoia." She agonized over this relationship; sometimes she ate, but more often she cried. She lived in this relationship the same way she had with food: swearing off every Monday. She achieved perfect abstinence during the week by transferring her obsession to workaholism. Monday through Friday, she was content to be "broken up" with him and refused his phone calls and invitations. By Friday, instead of heeding the "HALT" warning, she was too "horny, angry, lonely, and tired" and gave him another chance, bingeing on abuse for the weekend. After months of the same scenario, Ali's sponsor tired of the painful repetitions and advised her that she could no longer listen to these trials and tribulations. "Look Ali, I love you and it hurts me to hear this pain. I don't want to see you humiliated. You may have to go through this for yourself right now, but I can't listen anymore. Please call me with anything else you'd like to discuss, but I can't bear hearing what he does to you." Rather than give up the guy, Ali changed sponsors.

After months of "more of the same," Ali was at last finished with her suffering and told the man, "The pain of being with you is greater than the pain of being without you. I'm willing to bear this loss." She went to O.A. meetings all weekend. Within two months Mr. Wrong had found a young girl, a recent emigré from eastern Europe, and married her. This girl gained sixty pounds within six months! She, too, needed to eat compulsively to tolerate such abuse. Ali could have stayed in this abusive relationship if she had chosen to keep bingeing. Ali's only problem was that she wanted abstinence as well as that relationship. But she could not stay abstinent while being put down. Bingeing, we can endure anything: when we are abstinent we demand better treatment.

MENACING MENTORS

Mr. Wrong can also be found in the workplace. It often happens that an overeater who was able to maintain a consistently contented work situation during bingeing days discovers recovery brings problems on the job. Some even get fired! The work climate changes when the abstinent overeater will no longer tolerate degradation on the job. Many remained in abusive work situations simply because they felt secure that no one would confront them about their fat. Perhaps at work they were appreciated and never challenged. While bingeing, overeaters will do practically anything to avoid conflict. That often translates to living up to others' expectations rather than our own. A people-pleasing overeater will do anything to be liked.

This was Arnold's case as he sought to be loved in the marketplace. Mr. Rutledge had hired Arnold while he was still bingeing. Arnold's first paycheck was for less than what had been negotiated. Mr. Rutledge said he had made a mistake and could not negotiate a higher salary, but he would work on it. This first betrayal and Arnold's silent compliance set the tone for the future. Promised raises were slow to come, and each one was accompanied by a drastically increased workload. At the same time, Arnold's binge and withdrawal cycles became more and more numerous. His irritability during the withdrawal stages became unmanageable as he repeatedly lost his temper. He did have legitimate gripes about being overworked and underpaid, but he was not able to find an effective way to express them. Guilty and scared, Arnold did not feel worthy enough to confront legitimate issues while bingeing. When his courage rose enough to speak up, he would gag it with a Twinkie or a sundae. Then, when the withdrawals started, he seized any minor irritation as cause for raising the roof. Later, guilty and ashamed over his outbursts, he retreated into passive compliance, hoping that his loss of control would be forgotten. Mr. Rutledge rarely mentioned the outbursts; he didn't have to. Arnold was his own stern judge and jury and drove himself mercilessly to regain the "love" he thought he'd lost.

It was an ideal situation for Mr. Rutledge. He got a hell of a lot of work out of Arnold and enhanced his own career at Arnold's expense. Arnold saw Mr. Rutledge as a friend and confidant because he tolerated the outbursts. Arnold was so guilty and grateful! When he had suggestions for organizational improvements, he told them to Mr. Rutledge rather than submitting his ideas via the company suggestion box. Mr. Rutledge presented Arnold's ideas, getting the credit and the prize money. Arnold accepted this as okay; he felt "put in his place."

This worked for years as long as Arnold kept confusing humility and humiliation. The last straw was over a training manual for their division. Arnold worked long hours with no overtime to get it done on time only to see the boss submit it with his own name on the report. Arnold snapped!

What had actually snapped was Arnold's binge/fast cycle. He had started going to O.A. six months before and, thanks to his abstinence, started feeling deserving, worthwhile, and guilt-free. He had no guilt over inappropriate outbursts. More important, he trusted his instincts. Without his bingeing, Arnold's body became a clear indicator of whether or not he was living correctly. As long as Arnold was eating he didn't mind Mr. Rutledge rarely, if ever, acknowledging his contributions; but with six months' abstinence, seeing "Frank Rutledge" on his proposal made his stomach turn. Following his initial nausea came a feeling of violation. Rather than revert to his old habit of excessive emotionalism, Arnold called his sponsor to get advice from someone personally uninvolved. Arnold's main concern at that point was his EGO. "After all," he thought, "why make a big deal of it? So what if he did put his name on it? Let him take credit; everyone here knows who really did the work. If I were a truly spiritual being, this wouldn't bother me." He tried to talk his sponsor into the same rationalizations. Arnold's sponsor wouldn't buy it. He asked, "What does your body say? The body does not lie. If you are abstinent, you can trust your body as a clear channel for your own personal message. Trust your instincts." That advice enabled Arnold to approach Mr. Rutledge calmly and confidently, telling him how violated he felt.

In the past, as long as Arnold had been scared and guilty, Mr. Rutledge was understanding and reassuring. Now it was different. This time Arnold was confident, as well as abstinent, and it was Mr. Rutledge who became vicious and abusive, using all the information he had on Arnold in an attempt to keep him "one down" in the discussion: "How can you think you deserve credit for this report when I'm the one who taught you everything you know? Why, you wouldn't be here at all if it weren't for me. I MADE you, Arnold. You're getting too big for your britches since you started going to those meetings. You've got to be humbled, and I'll be the one to do it!" Arnold was aghast at this tirade but clearly saw the fear in the man standing before him. "Mr. Rutledge," he quietly replied, "that's not your job. I don't seek humility in the marketplace."

Interestingly enough, Mr. Rutledge really did believe he had "made" Arnold and when Arnold wanted credit for his own achievements, felt betrayed to the point that Arnold was fired within a month. Arnold subsequently developed his own consulting firm where he does get credit for his own work. Mr. Rutledge has never acknowledged Arnold's contribution and remains enraged at the one-time student and protege who stood up to him.

Many people in recovery have similar conflicts. They are involved with people they once adored and tried to emulate but with whom they now feel equality. Those perched on pedestals find it difficult to move over. Some teachers feel better with insecure and guilty pupils, thinking it enhances their self-image. Abstinence upsets this balance as recovering people begin to accept themselves and their own accomplishments instead of groveling. If overeaters were to stay "one down" while abstaining, they would return to eating to create an excuse for feeling bad. They wouldn't want to face the real issue lest they wind up fired like Arnold! The abstinence is worth the initial disruption, for not only is Arnold now thin, he is also successful and secure in his own business.

SPONSORS INSPIRE

Some need to exercise caution in choosing confidants within the program. There are those people who seek humiliation *within the program* by choosing confidants who can hurt them. If you do choose abuse, it is because you still expect it in your life. When the student is ready, the teacher appears. It is wise to consider carefully what you share from the podium. Some people can use the public lectern as a way to continue degrading themselves. Some things are best left for private discussions with your sponsor between meetings. Ask your sponsor's guidance regarding delicate material. We seek humility, not humiliation. Sexuality can become an issue in a recovery program. You could date indiscriminately within the fellowship as a way to continue feeling used and abused. Part of you could be trying to rationalize your way out of O.A. Since a large part of overeating has to do with excessive sexual appetite coupled with a distorted sexual attitude, it is best to choose guidance from those of your own sex who have felt similar feelings. This also dispels any flirting games in recovery. Most people in O.A. recommend that men sponsor men and women sponsor women.

Caution is necessary in choosing a sponsor in Twelve Step programs. If you come from a lifetime of humiliation and degradation, your tendency might be to seek people who still need to put others down. Despite your willingness to work the O.A. program, you must consider whether you are using your sponsor as another source of humiliation. O.A. is a fellowship of people who are first united by their common sickness and need. Some may seek ego glorification within the fellowship and begin helping others before they have worked through their own power and control needs. This is called "the O.A. two-step." It is a waltz from Step One to Step Twelve.

Many who are excellent speakers from the podium have great difficulty with intimacy on a personal level. As they brag about their entourage of "babies," they seem to be forever giving orders and ultimatums to those they sponsor. The directives are usually well-intentioned and represent the best knowledge the sponsor has at that moment.

We must trust our instincts: if we feel we've been violated, we probably have been. Even when a sponsor tells us things we don't want to hear, it can be done in a way that does not stab us in the heart. We might feel uncomfortable, argumentative, even disliked; but we won't feel worthless or bad. We will feel as though we are receiving information and direction. We will feel that someone else has experienced what we are going through, and that we are being treated with care and consideration while being nudged out of denial and into new growth. When we are truly getting help, truth, and direction, we will not feel worse about ourselves. We are already too good at beating ourselves up! A good guideline to follow is, "Love without honesty is sentimentality, but honesty without love is brutality."

A DOLL'S HOUSE RELATIONSHIP

Just because we have entered a recovery program and are concerned about our dignity does not mean that others in our lives will necessarily see our new needs. We may, in fact, find ourselves shocked by behavior we had once come to expect from others. They may continue the same old abuse, but now we will feel appalled and surprised. They may criticize us, "You seem extremely sensitive lately." Actually, with our weight loss, our vulnerable thinner skin has come to the surface.

Corrine and John had what they thought was an idyllic relationship. Family therapists refer to their interaction as a "doll's house marriage." The unwritten personal contract was based on the myth of man as a strong, macho decision maker; and woman as a confused, passive follower of directions. Their situation worked quite well as long as Corrine vomited twelve times a day. Because of the vomiting she was able to remain passive, frail, childlike, and adoring of her law student groom. All their friends commented on what a "cute couple" they were. It was as if they had walked off the top of their wedding cake into an applauding crowd of well-wishers. When Corrine entered recovery she was stoop-shouldered, waif-like, and her voice squeaked like a little girl's. "No one must ever know about my problem," she insisted. Her reputation was worth more to her than her life.

As her bingeing and purging subsided, Corrine wanted a separation from John. She found she could do quite well in recovery until she was around him; then she felt irritable and enraged. As long as she could stuff her rage down with food and vomit it back out, she could stay calm and relaxed (actually drugged and submissive). She liked this role; it fit her image of herself. But without her compulsive eating, it was not who she really was.

The young couple did separate for a few months and Corrine's vomiting subsided to a few slips, usually when she

17

talked with John on the telephone. Eventually, she was able to tolerate his phone calls without bingeing. Corrine was growing quickly and becoming stronger and stronger in recovery, and it was beginning to look like the relationship could work without food abuse. She developed a supportive group of friends so that she didn't need John in this role. For the first time in her life she got a job and found she enjoyed the independence of making her own way in the world. She felt good enough about herself to invite John to share this new security and freedom from food with her. She invited him to dinner, anxious to show him the new place she'd furnished on a simple budget with her own creative ideas.

John was late and belligerent from the beginning. He gave a cursory glance at the decor and barked, "I'll bet you forgot to make dinner reservations." Corrine just smiled and said, "No, I didn't forget and it's my treat." "Whose name are they in?" he asked. "We both have the same name, sweetheart," she smiled. John roared back, "Not if you don't shape up!" The situation progressed from bad to worse. Corrine talked about herself and her new projects; John told her she was "obsessed with herself." She asked about his life and he answered, "What can I be doing while you're so busy running around with weirdos?"

At the end of the evening, John revealed his motive in making the dinner date. "Look," he said, "you've had some fun these last few months. You've indulged yourself, but now it's time to come home. You're confused and you've let a bunch of people brainwash you. It's time to pack up and go home — I've got a trailer outside. You know I take better care of you than anyone else could, so let's go." Corrine was shocked. She really couldn't believe he would consider making decisions for her life without consulting her. He always had before, but she'd never noticed.

Her shock reflected the naiveté of recovery. We expect others to move at the same rate we are moving. Giving up food abuse accelerated Corrine's growth; but John did not have any motivation to change a situation he liked. Corrine had liked it then too, as long as she could vomit, and maintain the illusion of herself as fragile and dependent. The truth is that she is strong and willful, and she was shocked when she saw this typical example of their former relationship. She had married him because of his "take care of business" attitude. John was always the initiator; Corrine, the responder. He knew of no reason to include her in his planning. John was surprised to get her refusal instead of her appreciation.

GIVING UP GETTING EVEN

Because of feeling so bad about the loss of control with food, many overeaters resolve to appear winners in all other areas of life. This false front has to dissolve in recovery. While they may fail at the weight loss game they make up for it by becoming tremendously successful in the world of business, politics, or other areas. They resolve to WIN at a very high level, and they do. They commit to high achievement to feel deserving. Unfortunately, many people surrounded by Cadillacs, jewelry, and mansions are unable to give themselves the one gift they truly desire: a thin and healthy body.

This was true of Max, a corporate executive who had worked his way up to vice president of marketing in a highly competitive organization. In a precarious field where reputations are lost in a day, Max showed himself to be a consistent winner. He stepped over the heads of many people, including some he considered friends, and rationalized, "It's a dog-eat-dog world." His favorite joke was, "My tombstone will read, 'Nobody got the best of him.' " Food is what got the best of him during nightly binges.

He had tried O.A. once, but found the people too naive. "Maybe that 'turn it over' stuff works at home, but it sure doesn't apply in the marketplace. There you've got to plan and push and scheme or you'll drop by the wayside. You also have to be careful that no one takes advantage of you. Be suspicious and don't give anything away for free. If you're ever deceived by anyone, don't get mad, GET EVEN!"

That was his philosophy at the time he surrendered for the umpteenth time. He told his secretary he was going back to O.A. and declared he was swearing off "carbs." He planned to weigh and measure all food, call his sponsor, and follow directions. "This time," he said, "I'm really ready. I've hit bottom! When my sponsor says 'jump,' I'll ask 'how high?' on the way up!" He retreated into his office, arms full of O.A. pamphlets and a small notebook for his written food plan. He hoped that letting others in on his firm resolve would help keep him committed.

It was all over that same evening. He changed his mind on what he had contracted with his sponsor. He wanted to skip a meal, a sure setup for bingeing. His willing attitude had turned into a snarl as he defied anyone to contradict his plan to skip dinner. "I'm not hungry and I'm very busy. I just don't feel like eating and I'm not going to!" His secretary sat quietly. Within a twelve-hour period Max had given it all up. Max was looking for power and control.

What had happened to remove resolve and dash commitment? When Max had become reabsorbed in business, he had resorted to the same *winning* mentality that worked so well with his work but not with eating. By dinnertime he had tried to take control again and started to sing the O.A. dropout theme song, "I'll do it my way." His afternoon business behavior signaled the slip he would be into by evening.

A friend dropped by to tell of a new business venture. Max was critical and demanding, berating the friend for being foolish in not pushing for a lower price. Even though no one asked for any advice from Max, he insisted on giving it. He went into convoluted explanations of the ins and outs of transactions to save, at most, eighty dollars. It was as if his own abstinence was worth eighty dollars. His friend was not even very interested. The deal had already been set, and Max was there to share the good news. Though the friend was not in O.A., he worked from a fairly simple O.A. maxim: K.I.S.S., Keep It Simple, Sweetheart. Max did not want to stop there. "At least work it out so it will stay off the books and beat Uncle Sam out of the taxes." By working to beat the system, Max is trying to get away with something. Despite Max's belief that no one gets the best of him, his eating disorder does it every time. It is just a few short steps from getting away with something to believing that there is such a thing as a free lunch. As overeaters, we really believe we can overeat with impunity. Surrender is our only option.

The degree to which people like Max must aggressively win and make sure they are protected is in direct proportion to their loss of control over food. Since their best friend, FOOD, has turned on them, they would rather fight out the many minor skirmishes in life. The excessive zealousness to win triggers binge eating, which creates low self-worth.

WHEN WE SURRENDER, WE WIN

In recovery, we will have to lose to win. When we let go of the minor skirmishes, we can mobilize our forces for the greater battles ahead. If we are to remain abstinent, we must surrender the lesser prizes to achieve our real goal, recovery from our illness. Our egos may have to appear to lose for us to be true winners. We can walk away from degrading situations with dignity, knowing our real assets and liabilities. This is not humiliation; it's abstinence and humility.